Ripley's Believe It or Not!®

Developed and produced by Ripley Publishing Ltd

This edition published and distributed by:

Mason Crest
450 Parkway Drive, Suite D, Broomall, PA 19008
www.masoncrest.com

Printed and bound in the United States of America

First printing
9 8 7 6 5 4 3 2 1

Ripley's Believe It or Not!
Believe It!
ISBN: 978-1-4222-2773-2 (hardback)
ISBN: 978-1-4222-9034-7 (e-book)
Ripley's Believe It or Not!—Complete 8 Title Series
ISBN: 978-1-4222-2979-8

Cataloging-in-Publication Data on file with the Library of Congress

PUBLISHER'S NOTE
While every effort has been made to verify the accuracy of the entries in this book, the
Publishers cannot be held responsible for any errors contained in the work. They would
be glad to receive any information from readers.

WARNING
Some of the stunts and activities in this book are undertaken by experts and should not
be attempted by anyone without adequate training and supervision.

Strikingly True

BELIEVE IT!

www.MasonCrest.com

BELIEVE IT!

Open up your eyes to things beyond belief!

Dare to look at these unimaginable stories.

Look out for the outlandish tattooed ladies, the

man with the longest ear hair, and the mouse

that was found trapped in a loaf of bread.

Stuntman Ses Carny inserts fishing hooks into his eyes and pulls down...

believe it!
Believe It or Not!®

Tim Cockerill, aka The Great Inferno, happily gargles hot molten lead until it cools and hardens into solid metal in his mouth. During the day, Tim is a zoologist at Cambridge University in the U.K.

When he is not working in the lab, or trekking through a jungle to study insects, Tim wows audiences with such stunts as heating his tongue with a blowtorch, swallowing fire, and hammering nails into his head. The Great Inferno has been amazing audiences for 15 years with his extremely painful-looking acts.

The Great Inferno

Tim on the blowtorch stunt:

"The blowtorch stunt is one of the most difficult of the fire-eater's stunts to perform. With a flame that burns at around 1600°C [2,900°F], there is no margin for error—any hesitation would result in a serious burn. There is no real secret here, but the trick is to come at the flame with confidence and respect. This is one stunt that is just as intimidating no matter how many times you perform it!"

Tim on the blockhead stunt:

"The Human Blockhead was invented in the 1930s by sideshow performer Melvin Burkhart, 'The Anatomical Wonder.' What you see is what you get with this stunt—a solid steel nail is hammered all the way into the face. This is not something to be tried by anyone—get the angle wrong and the nail would go straight through the skull and into the brain!"

High Horse

From the 1880s through to the 1970s, one of the most popular shows on the Steel Pier in Atlantic City, New Jersey, was the horse high dive. Highly trained horses, usually ridden by girls, would leap from heights of up to 60 ft (18 m) into a pool 10 ft (3 m) deep. Riders asserted at the time that the horses enjoyed diving, were excellent swimmers, and were never forced to jump. However, owing to public pressure, diving horse shows died out in the 1970s and only one show remains—in a scaled-down form—in New York, where a riderless horse named Lightning will jump 10 ft (3 m) into water for a bucket of oats.

lottery luck Since 1993, Joan Ginther of Las Vegas, Nevada, has won the Texas Lottery four times, each time scooping at least $1 million, with total prize money of more than $20 million. She bought two of her winning tickets at the same store in Bishop, Texas, while visiting her father. Her chances of winning four lottery jackpots were put at more than 200-million-to-one.

classroom relic In June 2010, while cleaning up her classroom before a move, schoolteacher Michelle Eugenio of Peabody, Massachusetts, discovered a colonial-era document dating back to April 1792 among a pile of old books and scraps of paper.

dump dig Sanitation workers in Parsippany, New Jersey, dug through 10 tons of trash at a city dump to successfully recover a wedding ring that had been accidentally thrown away by a couple. Bridget Pericolo had placed the ring in a cup, but her husband of 55 years, Angelo, mistakenly threw it out with the garbage before leaving for work.

spelling mistake The general manager of the Chilean mint was fired after the country's name was spelt incorrectly on thousands of coins. The 2008 batch of 50-peso coins bore the stamp CHIIE, but amazingly the spelling mistake was not spotted until late 2009.

roar deal A thief in Germany stole a circus trailer in November 2009, unaware that there was a five-year-old lion in the back. The vehicle was later abandoned with its engine running after crashing into a road sign. Police believe the driver may have panicked on hearing the lion—named Caesar—let out a hungry roar.

double take When Helen MacGregor was sent a 21-year-old postcard of the town in Yorkshire, England, where she grew up, she was amazed to see herself in the center of the photo as a toddler. A friend had sent her the postcard of Otley, unaware that the child pictured in the street scene was Miss MacGregor, then aged three.

mistaken identity The dead body of a 75-year-old man slumped over a chair on the balcony of his third-floor Los Angeles, California, apartment was left undisturbed for several days in October 2009 as neighbors thought it was a Halloween dummy.

money to burn A German snowboarder stranded in the Austrian Alps for six hours in February 2010 was rescued after attracting attention by setting fire to his money. Stuck 33 ft (10 m) above ground after the ski lift was switched off at dusk, Dominik Podolsky was finally spotted by cleaners as he burned the last of his euros.

incriminating evidence An 18-year-old from Philadelphia, Pennsylvania, turned himself in to police in December 2009 for stealing a cell phone—after he took a photo of himself with it and it automatically sent a copy to the owner's e-mail!

close relatives Adopted by different families at a young age, biological brothers Stephen Goosney and Tommy Larkin finally found each other nearly 30 years later—and discovered that for the past seven months they had been living almost directly across the street from each other in Corner Brook, Newfoundland, Canada.

unexpected mourner Brazilian bricklayer Ademir Jorge Goncalves gave friends and family a surprise in November 2009 by turning up at his own funeral. Relatives had identified him as the disfigured victim of a car crash in Parana state, but actually he had been out on a drinking spree and did not hear about his funeral until it was already underway.

FACE PAINT

Lucky Diamond Rich is almost 100 percent covered with tattoos. Every inch of his skin is inked, including his eyelids and the insides of his ears. Lucky's incredibly dense face tattoos have developed over the last few years: He was last featured in *Ripley's Believe It or Not! Expect the Unexpected*, and his amazing transformation can clearly be seen. An international circus and street performer from Adelaide, Australia, Lucky has alloy-capped teeth with which he can perform extreme feats of strength.

Headless Chickens

In parts of Asia, no part of the chicken goes to waste. In Bangkok, the capital of Thailand, barbecued chicken head kebabs are available to buy as fast food. Once cooked, the brain and soft tissue can be eaten. Roasted, boiled, and deep-fried chicken heads are also popular.

slice of luck A restaurant in Hankou, China, selected from 15 applicants for the post of chef by asking the candidates to slice a melon on a woman's stomach. The successful candidate, Hu Gua, chopped up his melon in less than a minute without hurting the woman who was protected from the blade by just a thin sheet of plastic.

lime pie During the Key West, Florida, 2010 Conch Republic independence celebration, locals used 1,080 Key limes to prepare a 450-lb (204-kg), 7-ft-wide (2.1-m) Key lime pie.

taste test As a designer and tester with Fox's Biscuits, Simon Pope of West Yorkshire, England, is paid to eat more than 7,000 cookies a year.

margarine marge Restaurant owner Simon Smith of Staffordshire, England, celebrated the 20th birthday of *The Simpsons* by making a 4-ft-high (1.2-m) bust of his favorite character, Marge, out of margarine. He used 26 lb (12 kg) of special heat-resistant puff pastry margarine on the sculpture and achieved the shape by wrapping it around chicken wire.

chicken feast At the 2010 Canoefest in Brookville, Indiana, 1,654 lb (750 kg) of fried chicken was served up in a donated canoe. Up to 200 volunteers had cooked the 2,700 lb (1,225 kg) of raw meat.

cake tower Chef Gilles Stassart and architect Jean Bocabeille designed a cake for display in Paris, France, in July 2010 that was nearly 26 ft (7.8 m) tall—that's as high as a two-story house. The "Tower without Hunger" was made from 1,385 lb (628 kg) of flour, 1,120 lb (508 kg) of sugar, 350 eggs, and 40 lb (18 kg) of butter. The towering cake was meant to last four days outdoors but sweltering temperatures made it soft and unstable and it had to be taken down after just 24 hours.

haute dog New York City restaurant Serendipity 3 introduced a $69 hot dog in 2010. The Haute Dog comes with white truffle oil, a salted pretzel bed, truffle butter, duck foie gras, Dijon mustard, Vidalia onions, and ketchup.

locust topping When a plague of millions of locusts hit the town of Mildura, Victoria, Australia, in April 2010, pizza café owner Joe Carrazza put dozens of the dead insects on his pizzas as a topping.

placenta drink A new drink from Japanese health food manufacturer Nihon Sofuken tastes of peaches but contains 0.3 oz (10,000 mg) of pigs' placenta, a substance said to be able to restore youthful looks and help with dieting.

long fry John Benbenek of Buffalo, New York, was eating lunch at Taffy's Hot Dog Stand in 2010 when he found a 34-in-long (85-cm) French fry in his meal.

fiery sauce Eight teenagers in Augsburg, Germany, were treated in a hospital after a test of courage in which they drank chili sauce that was more than 200 times hotter than Tabasco. The sauce reached 535,000 on the Scoville scale, which measures the hotness of sauce, compared to 2,500 for normal Tabasco sauce.

bridge picnic More than 6,000 people sat down to breakfast on Sydney's famous Harbour Bridge in October 2009 after it was closed to traffic and carpeted with grass for a giant picnic.

double yolks Fiona Exon from Cumbria, England, beat odds of more than a trillion to one when she discovered that all six eggs she had bought in a single carton from her local grocery store had double yolks.

bacon envelopes U.S. company J & D's Foods, whose motto is "Everything should taste like bacon," have created "Mmmvelopes," envelopes that have a bacon flavor when you lick them.

chocolate landmark A team of Chinese confectioners built a 33-ft-long (10-m) replica of the Great Wall of China entirely out of chocolate. The wall was made of dark chocolate bricks held together by layers of white chocolate. It was unveiled at the 2010 World Chocolate Wonderland exhibition, which also featured 560 chocolate replicas of China's famous 2,200-year-old Terracotta Army.

giant pumpkin Christy Harp of Jackson Township, Ohio, took first place at the 2009 Ohio Valley Giant Pumpkin Growers' annual weigh-off with a pumpkin that weighed 1,725 lb (783 kg)—nearly ten times the weight of an average man. At one point her prizewinning pumpkin grew at a rate of 33 lb (15 kg) per day.

earthy taste Thuli Malindzi, 22, of Cape Town, South Africa, is addicted to eating soil and consumes a chunk every day. She has been eating earth for more than ten years and although she has tried to give up, she cannot resist hard lumps of clay, which she says taste like fudge.

salsa bowl During the 2010 Jacksonville Tomato Fest in Texas, a team of 20 volunteers made a 2,672-lb (1,212-kg) bowl of salsa.

1821 bun A hot cross bun baked on Good Friday, 1821, has been kept in a Lincolnshire, England, family for 190 years—and still shows no sign of mold. The fruity bun, which has the date March 1821 on its base, was made by Nancy Titman's great-great-great-grandfather, William Skinner, who owned a bakery in London. It was not eaten at the time and has been preserved in a box ever since, passed down through generations of the family as an unusual heirloom. The bun is now rock hard and the currants have disintegrated, but the shape of the cross is still visible.

PARTY BUG
Bug-eating parties are all the rage in Tokyo, Japan, where guests chow down on dishes such as grilled cockroaches, fried grasshoppers, cricket pie, and this red moth larvae soup.

chocolate wall To mark the 20th anniversary of the fall of the Berlin Wall, French chocolate-maker Patrick Roger constructed a 49-ft-long (15-m) replica of the landmark in chocolate. Over three weeks in 2009, he used 1,980 lb (900 kg) of chocolate to build the wall, and even added graffiti and artwork to the surface by spraying it with cocoa butter mixed with food coloring.

scorpion snack Li Liuqun of Hunan Province, China, is addicted to eating live scorpions and estimates he has eaten more than 10,000 over the last 30 years. Stung by a huge scorpion one day, he angrily bit off its head and enjoyed the taste so much that he now eats up to 30 in a single sitting. Luckily, he appears immune to the venom, which can paralyze and even kill people.

curry favor Feeding curry to sheep could help save the planet by lowering methane emissions. The spices used in curry kill the "bad" bacteria in a sheep's gut, reducing the amount of methane produced by up to 40 percent.

CREATIVE CAKES
Debbie Goard of Oakland, California, has created hundreds of incredibly lifelike custom-made cakes in the shape of animals, foodstuffs, and everyday objects. Her cake designs include dogs, a scorpion, a warthog, a burger, popcorn, spaghetti, sneakers, a Blackberry, a camera, and a baby giraffe that was nearly 2 ft (60 cm) tall. Her life-sized Chihuahua cake was so realistic that restaurant patrons were concerned there was a dog on the table!

BUOYANCY CASTLE

Three men from London, England, invented a
bizarre new water sport when they fulfilled an
ambition to ride a full-sized bouncy castle across
Lake Garda in Italy in May 2010. After drifting into
the path of a sailing regatta and being redirected
by a police launch, adventurers Jack Watkins,
Chris Hayes, and Dave Sibley completed the 5-mi
(8-km) voyage in two hours.

KING BOARD
Californians Joe Ciaglia and Rob Dyrdek built a giant skateboard that measures 36 ft 7 in (11.15 m) long, 8 ft 8 in (2.6 m) wide, 3 ft 7 in (1.09 m) tall, and weighs more than 3,600 lb (1,634 kg). It is 12 times larger than a standard board and is so big it is fitted with car tires and has to be transported on a flatbed truck.

maggot transfer In May 2009, Charlie Bell of London, England, moved 37½ lb (17 kg) of live maggots from one container to another—in his mouth. He practiced at home with rice for months before finally replacing the grains with the "revolting" maggots.

bike jump At Reno, Nevada, in 2009, U.S. motorcyclist Ryan Capes soared an astonishing 316 ft (96.3 m) through the air from one ramp to another.

secret stash Calin Tarescu of Alba Iulia, Romania, discovered that his wife had thrown away a pair of his old shoes in which he had stashed $64,000. Police helped him to recover the majority of the money.

hand stolen The mummified hand of a cheating gambler was stolen from a locked cabinet at a pub in Wiltshire, England, in March 2010. The hand, said to have been cut off a gambler caught cheating at the card game whist, was clutching a pack of 18th-century playing cards and is rumored to be cursed.

yoga queen At the age of 83, Bette Calman of Williamstown, Victoria, Australia, still teaches up to 11 yoga classes per week. She can perform headstands, "bridges," and, from lying on her front, can raise her whole body off the ground, using only her arms.

mighty pen Three men in Hyderabad, India, have created a pen that is not only mightier than a sword but is the size of a giraffe! The brass pen, which cost more than $5,000 to make, stands 16 ft (4.9 m) tall, 1 ft (30 cm) wide, weighs 88 lb (40 kg), and is embossed with Indian cultural illustrations.

buried alive After spending hours digging a 10-ft-deep (3-m) tunnel at a beach on Tenerife in Spain's Canary Islands, a 23-year-old German tourist had to be rescued when the sand collapsed and buried him up to his head. He was trapped on the beach for nearly two hours before 15 firefighters were able to free him.

free-fall solution After jumping from an airplane at an altitude of 14,000 ft (4,300 m), Ludwig Fichte of Dresden, Germany, flew through the air while sitting in a rubber dinghy and solving a Rubik's Cube puzzle. It took him 31.5 seconds during a free-fall descent of 5,900 ft (1,800 m) to solve the cube, at which point he deployed his parachute.

late appointment Reynolds Smith Jr. was appointed by the Alabama Democratic Party to sit on a party panel in October 2009—even though he had died 11 months earlier!

BUDDHIST MONK

Thai Buddhist monk Loung Pordaeng died in 1973, but to this day remains sitting in the Lotus position, the very position in which he died—naturally mummified in a temple on the Thai island of Koh Samui. Two months before he died at the age of 79, Loung believed his death to be imminent and asked that if his body did not decompose could it stay on display in the temple to inspire future generations to follow Buddhism. He meditated in silence for the final week of his life, eating and drinking nothing, and when he died his wishes were carried out. Local monks added a pair of sunglasses when his eyes eventually fell into his head.

ANCIENT TATTOOS

In 2006, a 1,500-year-old, heavily tattooed, and very well-preserved female mummy was discovered in a mud-brick pyramid in northern Peru. She was buried with many weapons, leading experts to believe that she could have been a rare warrior queen of the warlike Moche people.

BABY MUMMY

This incredibly well-preserved, mummified body of a young Peruvian child, who died some 6,500 years ago, is one of the oldest mummies ever found, and is hundreds of years older than the earliest known Egyptian mummies. It formed part of the largest collection of mummies ever assembled, which went on display at the California Science Center in Los Angeles in 2010.

®RIPLEY RESEARCH

Mummification—where skin, soft flesh, and hair remain on the bones—can preserve the human body for thousands of years. It can be achieved intentionally, such as with the elaborate Egyptian embalming ritual where the organs are removed from the body, or it can occur completely naturally. Natural mummification generally requires a dry atmosphere and a lack of oxygen to keep the natural process of decay at bay.

EGYPTIAN CAT

The ancient Egyptians, who practiced mummification on royal personages, also mummified animals. These underwent the same elaborate treatment as human corpses, with cloth wraps, a large amount of salt, and resin. This Egyptian cat is more than 2,000 years old.

THE ICE MAIDEN OF AMPATO

The frozen, mummified body of a teenage Incan girl was discovered near the 20,700-ft (6,310-m) summit of Mount Ampato, Peru, in 1995. It is thought that she was ritually sacrificed more than 500 years ago. Other mummified children have also been found on the mountain. The "Ice Maiden," as she is known, was removed from the site and is kept under controlled conditions in a Peruvian museum.

Mummies

ANCIENT BEAUTY

In 1934, a Swedish archeologist discovered hundreds of ancient mummies buried under boats in a mysterious cemetery in a remote desert in the Xinjiang region of China. The location, which featured rivers and lakes thousands of years ago, was lost until 2000, and researchers began to excavate the area in 2003. They found the body of a woman thought to have died almost 4,000 years ago, who has become known as the most beautiful mummy in the world, owing to incredibly well-preserved features that even include her eyelashes.

gold rush A huge 220-lb (100-kg) Canadian gold coin was sold at auction to a Spanish company for $4 million in 2010. One of only five $1 million Maple Leaf coins ever produced by the Royal Canadian Mint, it measures 21 in (53 cm) in diameter and is 1¼ in (3 cm) thick.

changing fortunes Brothers Zsolt and Geza Peladi were homeless and living in a cave outside Budapest, Hungary, when they discovered in December 2009 that they were due to inherit part of their grandmother's multi-billion euro fortune.

dummy guard In July 2010, two prisoners escaped from a jail in Argentina that, because of a lack of resources, was using a dummy to man one of its guard towers. Staff had put a prison officer's cap on a football to try to fool the convicts into thinking they were being watched from the tower by a real person.

blood match Eight years after breaking into a house in rural Tasmania, Australia, Peter Cannon was convicted of armed robbery because his DNA matched that of blood found inside a leech at the scene of the crime.

PIGLET BANK

An Internet site is selling a piggy bank made from a real piglet! The brainchild of designer Colin Hart from Belfast, Northern Ireland, the taxidermied pig with a slot in its back costs $4,000 and must be ordered 12 months in advance.

picture perfect When Royal Dutch Navy sergeant Dick de Bruin lost his camera while scuba diving off the Caribbean island of Aruba, he thought he would never see it again. However, seven months later the camera was found 1,130 mi (1,800 km) away by a coastguard at Key West, Florida—and although it was covered in crusty sea growth, it still worked.

remote patrol Burglars who broke into a man's apartment in Midwest City, Oklahoma, were caught via webcam by the man's wife more than 8,000 mi (12,875 km) away in the Philippines. Jim and Maribel Chouinard used the webcam to communicate face-to-face when they were apart.

old student A woman in China became an elementary school pupil at age 102. Ma Xiuxian from Jinan, Shandong Province, started work in a cotton mill at age 13 but had always longed for a proper education. So in 2010—89 years after leaving school—the grandmother went back, joining the grade one class at Weishan Road Elementary School. She uses hearing aids to make sure she can hear the teacher and a magnifying glass to help read text books.

frozen assets In May 2010, the Iowa Court of Appeals ordered the family of Orville Richardson, who died in February 2009 at age 81, to exhume his body so that his head could be cut off and frozen. In 2004, he had signed a contract with an Arizona company and paid $53,500 to have his head placed in cryogenic suspension after his death, but his siblings had buried him instead.

GO SLOW

Road safety campaigners in Canada encouraged motorists to reduce their speed by painting a large 3-D image of a child on to the road outside an elementary school in West Vancouver, British Columbia. The picture of a girl chasing after a ball appeared to come alive when drivers were 100 ft (30 m) away, giving them time to slow down.

ant arsonists A 2009 house fire in Daytona Beach, Florida, was started by ants. Dozens of carpenter ants had built their nest around an electrical box and, when the insects came in contact with the live wiring, they ignited. The resulting flames burst out of the box, set fire to an adjacent desk, and then spread to the rest of the house.

dead candidate Carl Robin Geary Sr. was elected mayor of Tracy City, Tennessee, on April 13, 2010, several weeks after he had died.

parallel lives Identical twins Jim Lewis and Jim Springer from Ohio were separated a month after birth, then reunited at age 39. Both had divorced a Linda, married a Betty, had sons named James, driven blue Chevrolets, and owned dogs named Toy.

lennon's toilet A toilet once owned by Beatle John Lennon was sold for the grand sum of $14,740 in 2010. The builder who had removed the lavatory from Lennon's Berkshire, England, home in 1971 kept it in his shed for almost 40 years.

granny auction Ten-year-old Zoe Pemberton of Essex, England, put her grandmother Marion Goodall up for sale on eBay in 2009, describing her as "cuddly" but "annoying." Although the listing was meant as a joke, bidding for the granny reached $30,000 before the auction website took it down.

soap drama A wife from Pune, Maharashtra, India, divorced her husband in August 2009 on the grounds that his refusal to allow her to watch her favorite soap operas on TV amounted to a form of domestic cruelty.

Long Hair

▸ When Tran Van Hay from Vietnam died in February 2010 his hair measured 22 ft (6.7 m) in length and weighed more than 23 lb (10.5 kg). He had not cut his hair for 50 years.

▸ Sardar Pishora Singh from India spent eight years cultivating a 3½-in-long (9-cm) eyebrow hair.

▸ When measured in 2004, Chinese Xie Quiping's hair measured 18 ft (5.5 m) in length. It had been growing for over 30 years without a trim.

▸ Justin Shaw from Miami has hair on his arms that measures 5¾ in (14.6 cm) in length.

▸ Brian Peterkin-Vertanesian from Washington, D.C., has a bizarre single eyebrow hair that has grown to more than 6 in (15 cm) in length.

▸ When Wesley Pemberton of Texas measured his leg hair in 2007, one of them was 6½ in (16.5 cm) long.

▸ Badamsinh Juwansinh Gurjar grew his mustache for 22 years, until it reached a length of 12½ ft (3.8 m).

▸ Norway's Hans Langseth died in 1927 with a beard that measured 17½ ft (5.3 m).

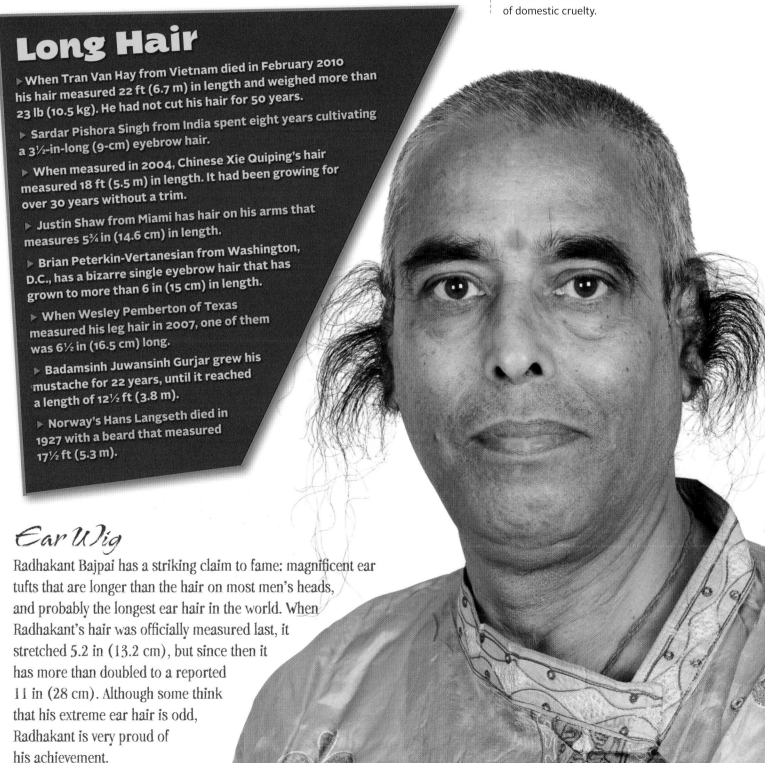

Ear Wig

Radhakant Bajpai has a striking claim to fame: magnificent ear tufts that are longer than the hair on most men's heads, and probably the longest ear hair in the world. When Radhakant's hair was officially measured last, it stretched 5.2 in (13.2 cm), but since then it has more than doubled to a reported 11 in (28 cm). Although some think that his extreme ear hair is odd, Radhakant is very proud of his achievement.

Ripley's
Believe It or Not!®

SERPENT QUEEN

While working for Ringling Bros. Circus in the 1880s, petite American Millie Betra, billed as the "Serpent Queen," regularly handled dozens of huge pythons that were almost twice her size, even wrapping many of the snakes around her body simultaneously.

WITH RINGLING BROS.'

Millie Betra, WORLD'S GREATEST SHOWS.

THE SERPENT QUEEN.

PHOTOGRAPHER.

J. V. Brown,

Milwaukee.

Completely Hooked

Massachusetts stuntman Ses Carny, "the American Madman," entertains audiences by inserting two stainless-steel fishing hooks into his eyes. With the sharp hooks resting on the orbital bones at the base of the eyes, he then pulls down on the hooks to reveal what it looks like under his eyeballs!

top of the world Jordan Romero of Big Bear Lake, California, reached the summit of Mount Everest in May 2010—at the age of just 13. He climbed with his father and three Sherpa guides, and on getting to the peak of the world's highest mountain he telephoned his mother and said: "Mom, I'm calling you from the top of the world." Jordan has conquered many of the world's highest mountains, and climbed Africa's Mount Kilimanjaro when he was only ten.

limbo queen Shemika Charles from Buffalo, New York State, weighs 140 lb (63.5 kg) and stands 5 ft 9 in (1.75 m) tall, but can limbo under a bar just 8½ in (22 cm) off the ground—while carrying a tray with three fuel canisters in each hand.

happy meals Kelvin Baines of Devon, England, began his collection of McDonald's Happy Meal toys in the 1980s and he now has more than 7,500.

rubber bands Allison Coach, 11, from Chesterfield Township, Michigan, has created a rubber band chain that measures more than 1.3 mi (2.1 km) long. She keeps the chain, which consists of more than 22,000 rubber bands, wrapped around a wooden stand made by her grandfather.

clog dance More than 2,500 people in Pella, Iowa, took part in a mass clog dance in May 2010. To ease the discomfort of the wooden shoes they were wearing, many of the dancers put on extra-thick socks or stuffed their clogs with sponges.

blind speedster Turkish pop singer Metin Senturk drove a car at 182 mph (292.9 km/h)—even though he is blind. He drove a Ferrari F430 unaccompanied along the runway at Urfa airport, with a co-driver giving him instructions through an earpiece in his helmet from a car following behind.

giant clock The family clock-making firm Smith of Derby, England, built a huge mechanical clock 42 ft 8 in (13 m) in diameter with a minute hand 25 ft 7 in (7.8 m) long. The 11-ton clock took a year to design and build and was delivered to its final home—in Ganzhou, China—in 2010 for installation in the 371-ft-high (113-m) Harmony Tower.

cucumber man Frank Dimmock, 87, from Oxfordshire, England, grew a cucumber 41¼ in (104.8 cm) long in 2010. Known as the "Cucumber Man," he has been growing vegetables since before World War II when he became an apprentice to a gardener.

tower leap In May 2010, Algerian-born rollerblader Taig Khris leaped from the 131-ft-high (40-m) first floor of Paris's Eiffel Tower and landed safely onto a 98-ft-high (30-m) ramp.

GREAT BALL OF FIRE

Pilot Captain Brian Bews parachuted to safety seconds before his $30-million CF-18 fighter jet crashed and exploded in a devastating ball of fire at Lethbridge County Airport, Alberta, Canada. Having completed his practice routine for the 2010 Alberta International Air Show, he was returning to land at the airport when the plane suddenly nose-dived on approach. Just 100 ft (30 m) from the ground, he managed to escape using the plane's rocket-powered ejector seat. Moments later, the plane smashed into the ground and was engulfed in smoke and flames, but Captain Bews survived with only minor injuries.

CHEATED DEATH

Stunt pilot Dino Moline cheated death by a split second by deploying his built-in parachute after a wing of his plane fell off at an air show in Santa Fe, Argentina. After performing a series of daring, acrobatic maneuvers, Moline was flying upside down when he felt an explosion and saw the shadow of the detached wing pass the cockpit. As the plane spiraled out of control, he instantly activated its parachute, which slowed the aircraft's descent and allowed it to float gently to the ground where it caught fire. Moline escaped with only one small injury—a burned foot.

GLIDER CRASH

Former racing-car driver Mike Newman escaped unharmed except for three broken vertebrae after the glider he was piloting crashed at high speed into the runway in front of 15,000 spectators at an air show in West Sussex, England. After performing his routine, he prepared to land but a malfunction caused the glider to plunge almost vertically to the ground, striking its wing first. The nose section crumpled around him and the cockpit burst open, leaving him dangerously exposed. He lay stunned amid the wreckage for a minute before managing to stumble out onto the runway.

Ripley's Believe It or Not!®

FAITHFUL FEET

Hua Chi, a monk at a monastery near Tongren, China, has been coming to exactly the same spot to kowtow at the temple for so many years that perfect footprints have been worn into the wooden floor. For nearly 20 years he has carefully placed his feet to bend down, and lie prostrate, two- to three-thousand times a day, although now that he's over 70 years old, he can manage only a thousand!

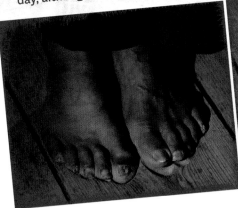

four babies
Four sisters from one family each gave birth within four days in 2010. The same obstetrician delivered the babies of Lilian Sepulveda, Saby Pazos, and Leslie Pazos at the same Chicago, Illinois, hospital on August 6 and 7, and a fourth sister, Heidi Lopez, gave birth in California on August 9.

200 grandkids
During her life, Yitta Schwartz (1917–2010) of Kiryas Joel, New York, had 15 children, more than 200 grandchildren, and a staggering total of more than 2,000 living descendants.

WORKING FLAT OUT

Hurrying to impose new parking restrictions ahead of the 2010 Tall Ships sailing races, council workers in Hartlepool, England, painted yellow lines right over a squashed, dead hedgehog in the road rather than move the animal.

cash bonfire
Infamous Colombian drug baron Pablo Escobar once burned more than $1.5 million in cash to keep his daughter Manuela warm during a single night on the run. When he realized she was suffering from hypothermia at his mountain hideout, he lit a bonfire using wads of U.S. dollars.

extra time
A Thai man spent three extra years behind bars in an Indonesian prison because of a typo in his paperwork. Kamjai Khong Thavorn should have been released in 2007 after serving a 20-year sentence for possessing heroin, but a clerical error wrongly stated his first year in prison as 1997 instead of 1987. The error was not spotted until 2010.

fake workers
After adding biometric scanning to record employee attendance in 2009, the city of Delhi, India, discovered 22,853 fake workers on its payroll.

croc monsieur
After receiving reports of a 12-ft-long (3.6-m) crocodile circling boats in the English Channel, French authorities banned swimming near Boulogne and broadcast warnings to vacationers in both French and English—only to discover that the reptile was nothing more dangerous than a floating piece of wood.

satan image
A family in Budapest, Hungary, abandoned their new-look bathroom after an image of Satan appeared overnight in a tile. Emerging from her first shower in the freshly decorated room, Andrea Csrefko fled in horror when she noticed the horned head of the devil in one of the tiles. The spooky image had not been there when husband Laszlo had put the tiles up and no cleaning detergent was able to remove it.

what fire?
A man in Pittsburgh, Pennsylvania, slept while his house caught fire and part of the roof collapsed. It was not until fire crews did a walk-through of the house more than two hours later that he woke up.

document leak
A 2,400-page restricted document from Britain's Ministry of Defence giving advice on how to stop documents leaking onto the Internet was itself leaked onto the Internet in 2009.

unique stamp
The one-of-a-kind Treskilling Yellow postage stamp is worth about $7.4 million. First issued in Sweden in 1855, it owes its value to the fact that it was printed in yellow by mistake, when the rest of the batch was green. It survives today thanks only to a 14-year-old Swedish schoolboy who rescued it from his grandmother's garbage bin in 1885 and sold it to a dealer for about $1.

end of war
Although fighting in World War I finished in 1918, the war did not officially end until October 3, 2010—92 years later—when Germany finally settled its war debt by paying $90 million, which was the last instalment of the reparations imposed on it by the Allies. Germany was forced to pay compensation toward the cost of the war by the 1919 Treaty of Versailles—the bill would have been settled much earlier but Adolf Hitler reneged on the agreement.

High Tea

Waiters serve lunch to two steel workers perched on a girder high above New York City in 1930. The men were working on the construction of the 47-story, 625-ft-high (190-m) Waldorf-Astoria Hotel on Park Avenue.

delayed delivery Gill Smeathers of Northamptonshire, England, received a package in February 2010 that was postmarked November 4, 1982.

inflated numbers During World War II, the 1,100 men of the U.S. Army's 23rd Headquarters Special Troops used inflatable vehicles, sound recordings, and fake radio broadcasts to deceive the enemy into thinking they were an army of 30,000 soldiers.

mattress mishap After accidentally throwing away a mattress that her mother had stuffed with $1 million, a Tel Aviv woman searched in vain through Israeli landfill sites containing thousands of tons of garbage. She had bought her mother a new mattress as a surprise.

battle dead In 2010, Brian Freeman, a former Australian army captain, uncovered the forgotten site of a World-War-II battle in Papua New Guinea, with the bodies of three Japanese soldiers still lying where they fell in 1942. Local villagers led him to Eora Creek—the biggest single battle of the Kokoda campaign—where he found the remains of the soldiers, along with their weapons and equipment.

lucky numbers Beating astronomical odds, Ernest Pullen of Bonne Terre, Missouri, won $3 million in two separate lotteries in the space of three months. After picking up $1 million in June 2010, he won another $2 million in September, combining his lucky numbers with numbers he had dreamed about six years earlier when foreseeing that he would one day win a lot of money.

own phone After his cell phone was stolen, a Californian man bought a new one on classifieds website Craigslist, choosing it because it looked just like his old phone. When it arrived, it actually was his old phone and still had his numbers stored. Luckily for the police, the thief had put his return address on the package.

balloon daredevils Early balloonists used highly flammable hydrogen gas instead of hot air or helium. In 1785, the French inventor Jean-Pierre Blanchard and American John Jeffries used an early hydrogen gas balloon to fly across the English Channel between England and France. When Jean-François Pilâtre de Rozier attempted to do the same, his balloon exploded and he became the first to die in an air accident.

Believe It or Not!®

A Bug's Life

Artist Chris Trueman of Claremont, California, came up with an unusual way to make this portrait of his younger brother dressed up as a cowboy look like an old, yellowed photograph—he used 200,000 dead ants. At first Chris tried to catch the harvester ants himself, but he soon realized that it would take him years to catch enough for the painting. So, he bought the ants live over the Internet and, after killing them, incorporated their bodies into the painting with tweezers and a resin called Galkyd, which has a yellowish color. It took him about two weeks to apply each batch of 40,000 ants to the portrait. The painting was first exhibited at the Alexander Salazar gallery in San Diego, but is now owned by Ripley's and will soon be on display in one of Ripley's 32 museums worldwide.

Ripley's Ask

What is the story behind the original photograph? I staged and photographed my youngest brother Bryce when he was 6 or 7. I had him dress up in my old cowboy outfit and hold my father's unloaded rifle. He was in my parents' suburban backyard. It was a menacing image, as he pretended to be a cowboy, but was holding a real gun.

Why did you decide to use ants for the image? I was revisiting a specific experience from my childhood. When I was five years old, my younger brother and I attacked an anthill and were bitten by red ants. That was the first time I intentionally tried to harm intelligent life and, more than 25 years later, I decided to return to that experience. Ants ride the line of what we consider intelligent life—if we see them in the kitchen, many of us think little of killing them all. But if we take the time to look at them closely, they are remarkable creatures.

How long did it take to complete? It took several years, not because of the actual labor, but because at one point I started to feel bad about killing all of the ants and I stopped the project for over a year. Then I decided that because I was most of the way done, the first ants would have died in vain if I didn't finish the work, so I decided to continue. It was also quite an expensive work to produce as each shipment of ants would cost $500.

Can you explain how you work the ants into the painting? In the detailed areas I worked with tweezers and would put down a layer of Galkyd resin and then position the ants. In areas where the detail was less specific, I would sprinkle the ants on.

What was the most challenging aspect of this piece of work? The work was challenging from start to finish, finding and acquiring the ants, figuring out what medium to use, getting the right image, working in the details. I also had a hard time carrying through with the project. Some people don't believe me that it was hard to kill them, but I think at that quantity you become hyper-aware of what you are doing.

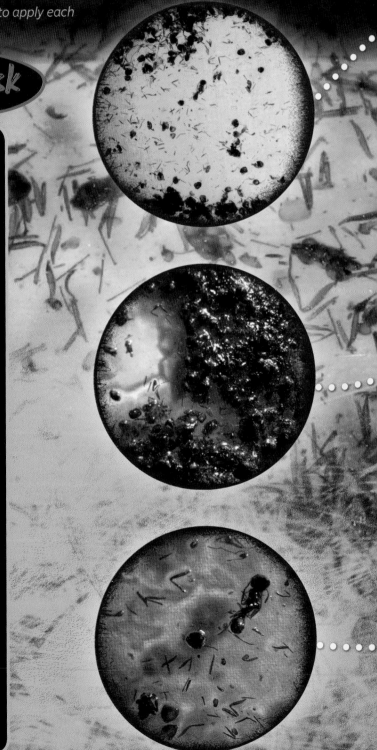

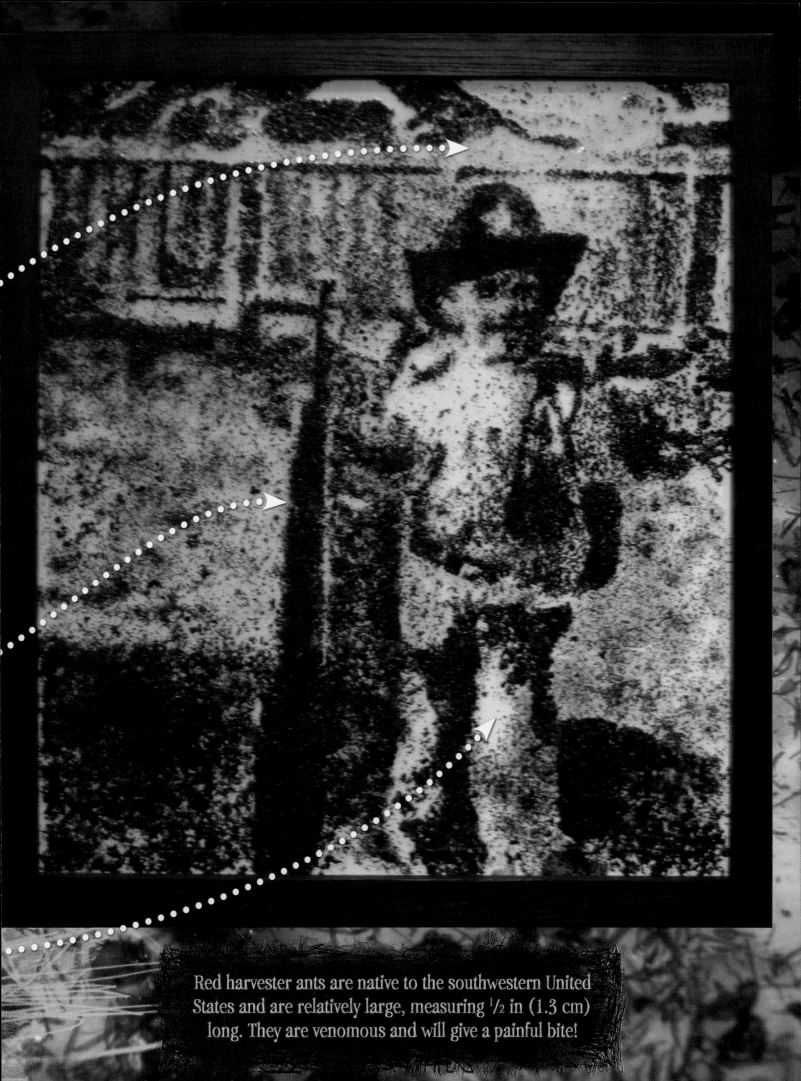

Red harvester ants are native to the southwestern United States and are relatively large, measuring ½ in (1.3 cm) long. They are venomous and will give a painful bite!

Nose for Trouble

An anti-landmine organization based in Belgium uses African giant pouched rats to sniff out deadly landmines in Mozambique and Tanzania. The rats' relatively light weight means they are unlikely to explode the mines, even when scratching at the ground to indicate their whereabouts. These super rats, trained with food rewards, can also smell the life-threatening disease tuberculosis, analyzing samples more than 50 times quicker than a laboratory scientist.

surprise visit After nine-year-old Beatrice Delap wrote to Captain Jack Sparrow—Johnny Depp's character in the *Pirates of the Caribbean* movies—asking for help with an uprising against teachers at her school in Greenwich, London, Depp responded by turning up at the school in full pirate costume. The Hollywood star was in the area filming the fourth movie in the series in October 2010 and gave the school 10 minutes' notice that he was on his way.

deadly shock A 70-year-old Indian man was so shocked to receive a bogus receipt for his own cremation service that he suffered a fatal heart attack. Horrified to read that he had supposedly been cremated the week before, dairy farmer Frail Than Singh collapsed with chest pains—and his body was subsequently delivered to the same crematorium in Ghaziabad and given the same serial number, 89, as listed on the fake letter.

unlucky number Superstitious phone company bosses in Bulgaria suspended a jinxed cell phone number—0888 888 888—in 2010 after all three customers to whom it had been assigned over the previous ten years suffered untimely deaths.

identical couples Identical twin brothers married identical twin sisters in a joint wedding ceremony in China. Grooms Yang Kang and Yang Jian sported different haircuts for the ceremony so that people could tell them apart, while brides Zhang Lanxiang and Jiang Juxiang wore differently colored dresses.

ghostly sale Two vials said to contain the spirits of ghosts exorcised from a house in Christchurch, New Zealand, were sold on an online auction site for more than $1,500 in March 2010. The sales pitch claimed that the "holy water" in the vials had dulled the spirits' energy and put them to sleep. To revive them, the buyer would need to pour the contents into a dish and let them "evaporate into your house." The seller, Avie Woodbury, said that once an exorcist's fee had been deducted, the proceeds of the spirit sale would go to an animal welfare group.

sold soul More than 7,000 online shoppers unwittingly agreed to sell their souls in 2010, thanks to a clause in the terms and conditions of a British computer-game retailer. As an April Fool's Day joke to highlight the fact that online shoppers do not read the small print, GameStation added a clause to its contract granting it a "non transferable option to claim, for now and for ever more, your immortal soul."

lucky seven On March 31, 2010, the four-number state lottery in Pennsylvania came up 7-7-7-7 and had a $7.77 million payout!

DEAD RINGER

Biker David Morales Colón of San Juan, Puerto Rico, became a dead ringer for his idol Meat Loaf by attending his own funeral in 2010 on the back of his beloved Honda motorcycle. So that friends could pay their respects at his wake, undertakers mounted his embalmed body carefully on the machine, hiding a series of body braces beneath his clothes and covering his eyes with wraparound sunglasses.

ruff justice In Athens, Georgia, a woman scared off a would-be burglar by acting like a dog. Police said she got on the floor and began scratching at the door and acting like a large dog when the intruder tried turning the door knob—he then ran away.

kept corpses Jean Stevens of Bradford County, Pennsylvania, lived with the corpse of her dead husband for ten years and with the body of her dead twin sister for almost a year. After they died, she had their embalmed bodies dug up and stored at her house. She maintained the immaculately dressed corpses as best she could, spraying sister June with expensive perfume and keeping her on a couch in a spare room while husband James rested on a couch in the garage.

frustrated caller A woman from Clarksville, Tennessee, was arrested in 2009 after she kept calling 911 to complain that a man refused to marry her.

OFF ROAD

Lin Su from China drove his brand new Subaru SUV 100 ft (30 m) into the sea from Sanya beach, Hainan Province, in 2010, before getting out and leaving his vehicle in the waves. He announced that the car was no longer needed, and that he had abandoned it as an offering to the Chinese dragon water god, to ask for respite for recent severe flooding. The Subaru was eventually salvaged from the sea by the police.

confused clergy Two female clerics at the same church in Cambridgeshire, England, share the same three names—Rhiannon Elizabeth Jones. Both are also graduates of the same college.

antique gown When three-month-old George Parfitt was baptized in Devon, England, in 2009, he wore the same antique christening gown that had been used by 20 members of his family since it was made by his great-great-great-grandmother in 1884.

lung stolen Organizers offered $2,000 for the return of a left lung that was stolen from a traveling exhibition of human cadavers in Peru in 2009.

BEARDED MOTHER

Richard Lorenc of Kansas finally tracked down his birth mother in 2010—and discovered that she is a famous bearded lady who as a young girl worked in a circus sideshow. Vivian Wheeler boasts an 11-in-long (28-cm) beard, as a result of inheriting the condition hypertrichosis, also known as werewolf syndrome, which causes the growth of excessive facial hair from an early age.

prize catch Barbara and Dennis Gregory of Johannesburg, South Africa, lost their camera when it dropped into the sea from the *Queen Mary 2* cruise ship en route from New York to Southampton in 2008. Sixteen months later, Spanish fisherman Benito Estevez found the camera in his nets and traced the couple after posting the photographs online.

cash stash Four children aged between 10 and 13 who found $20,000 stuffed in a brown envelope on their way to school in Frankfurt, Germany, shared it out among their friends in the playground. After teachers were alerted, police managed to recoup most of the cash.

grim find A Dutch riverboat captain who dropped anchor in the River Danube in Austria had a surprise when he raised it. He hauled up a BMW car—with the dead driver still behind the steering wheel.

prison landing A driver escaping from police officers in Cleveland, Ohio, abandoned his car after a 90-mph (145-km/h) chase and jumped a fence—only to land in the yard of the state women's prison where he was quickly arrested.

all the nines Henry Michael Berendes of Wisconsin was born at 9.09 a.m. on 9-9-09 and weighed 9 lb 9 oz (4.3 kg).

Ripley's Believe It or Not!®

Tattooed Ladies

The tattooed lady was an astonishing and beautiful addition to the circus sideshows, dime museums, and carnivals that were found in North America and Europe in the late 19th century. They featured in such shows until the late 20th century, when the last tattooed lady retired, aged 80, in 1995.

TRIBAL CUSTOM

The outlandish stories of Nora Hildebrandt and Irene Woodward (see far right) were perhaps based on the true tale of Olive Oatman. In 1850, as she traveled with her family in a wagon train, they were attacked by Yavapai Indians. She and her sister were the only ones to survive and were sold to the Mojave tribe, who treated Olive kindly but tattooed her chin in keeping with tribal custom. Olive was content with her captors and was reluctant to leave the Mojave tribe when she was "rescued" two years later.

Olive Oatman

Betty Broadbent

TATTOO BARGAIN

As a young girl, Lady Viola had made an agreement with her family that if she trained as a nurse she could do anything she liked afterward. Once qualified, she kept them to their word and got her first tattoo. Often billed as "The Most Beautiful Tattooed Woman in the World," Lady Viola's tattoos included the portraits of six U.S. presidents across her chest. The Capitol decorated her back, the Statue of Liberty and Rock of Ages her legs. During the outdoor season in the 1930s, she worked with the Ringling Brothers Circus, while winter months found her in dime museums, such as Gorman's in Philadelphia. She was still working at the age of 73.

Lady Viola

DISOWNED

Betty was born in 1909. During a girls' weekend in Atlantic City, New Jersey, she got a small tattoo and, as a result, her family disowned her. She claimed she had no other choice but to get more tattoos and make a career out of them. Betty worked with many circuses and was an attraction at the 1939 New York World's Fair with the "John Hix Strange as it Seems" sideshow.

INK REPELLANT

One of the first Western women to be significantly tattooed was Irene Woodward. On her debut in 1882, she scandalized the public with her tattoos, which had previously only been seen on sailors. Inked by her father, Irene maintained (probably not truthfully) that he did it to protect her from being captured by American Indians. Described on one show billboard as "A pretty picturesque specimen of punctured purity," she was a shy and dignified performer.

Irene Woodward

SHOCKING STORY

Every great tattooed lady had a sensational story, and Nora Hildebrandt dramatically claimed that she'd been forcibly tattooed by American Indians while tied to a tree for a year. She even said that Sitting Bull was involved in the murky affair. The truth was a little less scandalous— Nora's father tattooed soldiers fighting in the Civil War and used to practice his designs on his daughter. By the time she began to exhibit herself in 1882, she had 365 tattoos.

Nora Hildebrandt

MARRIAGE OF EQUALS

One night in July 1885, the audience at the Sells Brothers Circus in Burlington, Iowa, got a surprise. During the performance, tattooed Frank de Burgh came into the ring bare-chested to marry Emma Kohl, who wore a revealing costume that showed off her own wonderful designs.

Emma de Burgh

SNAKE CHARMER

In the late 19th and early 20th century, it was fashionable for aristocrats, including women, to be tattooed. Lady Randolph Churchill, Winston Churchill's mother, had a snake tattooed on her wrist. Tattoos then were very expensive. Later, as costs came down, tattooing was adopted by the lower classes and the practice fell out of favor with the social élite.

Ripley's Believe It or Not!®

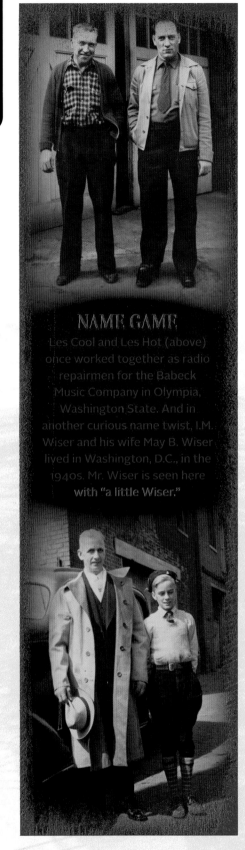

NAME GAME

Les Cool and Les Hot (above) once worked together as radio repairmen for the Babeck Music Company in Olympia, Washington State. And in another curious name twist, I.M. Wiser and his wife May B. Wiser lived in Washington, D.C., in the 1940s. Mr. Wiser is seen here with "a little Wiser."

small world In 1980, when Alex and Donna Voutsinas lived in different countries and long before they met and married, they were captured in the same photo at Walt Disney World, Orlando, Florida. Five-year-old Donna was photographed at the same moment as three-year-old Alex, who then lived in Montréal, Canada, was being pushed down Main Street in a stroller by his father.

same name In 2009, 77-year-old retired policeman Geraint Woolford was admitted to Abergele Hospital in North Wales and placed in a bed next to a 52-year-old Geraint Woolford, unrelated and also a retired policeman! The two men had never met before and checks showed they are the only two people in the whole of Great Britain named Geraint Woolford.

short journey Six-year-old Heidi Kay Werstler tossed a message in a bottle into the sea at Ocean City, New Jersey, in 1985 and it washed ashore 24 years later at Duck, North Carolina—less than 300 mi (480 km) away.

spoon dig A female convict used a spoon to dig her way out of a prison in Breda in the Netherlands, in February 2010. Using the spoon, she dug a tunnel under the cellar of the prison's kitchen to the outside world.

treasure trove A Scottish game warden who bought a metal detector for a new hobby struck gold on his very first treasure hunt, discovering a $1.5 million hoard of Iron-Age jewelry. Five days after taking delivery of the detector and just seven steps into his first hunt, David Booth unearthed four 2,300-year-old items made of pure gold—the most significant discovery ever of Iron-Age metalwork in Scotland.

force farce The entire police force in a Hungarian town quit after winning more than $15 million on the lottery in 2009. The 15-strong squad in Budaörs resigned immediately after scooping the jackpot.

shoe thief A second-hand shoe store owner stole more than 1,200 pairs of designer shoes by posing as a mourner at hospitals and funeral homes in South Korea. His victims were genuine friends and relatives of the deceased, who had slipped off their shoes in a traditional demonstration of respect. The thief would remove his own footwear, pay his respects, then put on a more expensive pair and walk off.

last post A postcard bringing holiday news to a couple in West Yorkshire, England, was delivered in 2009—40 years after it was posted.

family graduation Chao Muhe, 96, and his grandson Zhao Shuangzhan, 32, both graduated from university in June 2009. Retired lecturer Chao, who enrolled to set an example to his grandson, earned a master's degree in philosophy from the University of South China in Taiwan, while Zhao graduated from Chung Hua University. During the six-year course, Chao never missed a class despite needing to get up at 5 a.m. every day to catch several buses to the university.

vader raider In July 2010, a man robbed a bank in Setauket, New York State, dressed in the mask and cape of Darth Vader, the villain from the *Star Wars* movies.

bad timing At Lowestoft, Suffolk, England in 2010, an unlucky 13-year-old boy was struck by lightning at 13.13 on Friday, August 13. Thankfully, he suffered only minor burns and made a full recovery.

winner winner A store in Winner, South Dakota, sold the winning ticket, worth $232 million, in the drawing of the Powerball Lottery on May 27, 2009.

thumb find When fisherman Blake Robinson caught a 6½-lb (2.9-kg) lake trout at Flaming Gorge Reservoir, Wyoming, he discovered a human thumb inside it.

crushed crustacean A lobster became one of the last casualties of World War II when it was blown up inside an unexploded mine in 2009. The crustacean had made its home inside the 600-lb (272-kg) mine that had lay dormant on the seabed off the coast of Dorset, England, for more than 60 years—but when the Royal Navy's bomb disposal unit tried to coax it out before detonating the device, it refused to move and instead delivered a nasty nip to the divers.

watch returned A pocket watch was returned to the family of Welsh sailor Richard Prichard in 2009—128 years after his death. In 2000, diver Rich Hughes had been exploring the wreck of Prichard's ship—the *Barbara*—that sank in 1881, when he found the watch. After nine years of painstaking research, he was finally able to identify the owner's family and give the watch back.

Singing Ban With Venezuela suffering from serious water and energy shortages in 2009, the country's President Hugo Chavez ordered his citizens to stop singing in the shower. He hoped the ban would limit the amount of time people spent using water in the bathroom.

SWING THE LIZARD

As a change from roaming the grassland at India's Corbett National Park, an Indian elephant named Madhuri picked up a passing monitor lizard and played with it for several days. With the lizard's tail firmly grasped in her trunk, she carried it with her wherever she went, swinging it around in the air over and over again, sometimes tossing it high and even dropping it before finally letting the dazed reptile go.

Watch the Beardie

Charles Earnshaw of Anchorage, Alaska, displays his "Beards of a Feather" facial hair sculpture at the 2010 U.S. National Beard and Mustache Championships in Bend, Oregon. There were over 200 entrants, and this creation earned him a prize in the freestyle section.

Ripley's Believe It or Not!®

expensive bottle In London, England, in 2009, jeweler Donald Edge unveiled a gold, pearl, and diamond-encrusted bottle of Chambord raspberry liqueur that was valued at over $2 million. The bottle featured 1,100 individual diamonds.

banana bonanza Banana peels make up more than half of the trash collected on Scotland's Ben Nevis mountain. During a September 2009 survey, more than 1,000 discarded banana skins were found on the summit plateau.

chocolate coin Chocolatiers Gary Mitchell, Jess Nolasco, and Rita Craig, from Purdy's Chocolates, Vancouver, Canada, spent more than eight hours creating a 25-lb (11.3-kg) chocolate coin, measuring 24 in (60 cm) wide and 1½ in (4 cm) thick, and valued at $625.

fast food "Humble" Bob Shoudt from Royersford, Pennsylvania, won first prize of $2,500 for eating 7 lb 14½ oz (3.58 kg) of French fries in ten minutes at the Curley's Fries Eating Championship at Morey's Piers, Wildwood, New Jersey, in May 2010.

vintage cognac A French entrepreneur bought a bottle of Cognac dating back to 1788—the year before the French Revolution—for nearly $37,000 at a Paris wine auction in December 2009.

sushi roll In November 2009, hundreds of students at the University of California, Berkeley, assembled a 330-ft-long (100-m) sushi roll. They used 200 lb (90 kg) of rice, 180 lb (82 kg) of fish, 80 lb (36 kg) of avocado, and 80 lb (36 kg) of cucumber. To cater for vegetarians, the final 15 ft (4.5 m) contained tofu instead of seafood.

moon beer In its thirst to create even better beer, the family-owned Brewery Caulier in Péruwelz, Belgium, has begun producing beer made by the light of a full moon. The full moon speeds up the fermentation process, shortening it from seven days to five, which adds extra punch to the beer, giving it a stronger flavor.

triple yolker Bob Harrop from Devon, England, beat odds of 25 million to one when he found a triple-yolk egg while preparing his breakfast. The former hotelier has fried more than 155,000 eggs over the years and has seen hundreds of double yolkers, but this was the first time he had ever come across an egg with three yolks.

FAT DRAGON
Japanese-born pastry chef Naoko Sukegawa created a sculpture of a dragon made from margarine. The dragon, built over a steel and mesh frame, stood 29 in (74 cm) high, weighed 35 lb (16 kg), and took four months to make.

super potato Amateur gardener Peter Glazebrook of Northampton, England, grew a potato that weighed 8 lb 4 oz (3.74 kg)—the weight of a newborn baby and 25 times more than the weight of an average potato. The supersized potato would make 66 bags of potato chips, 33 portions of fries, 80 roast potatoes, or 44 portions of mashed potato.

pizza chain A chain of 2,200 pizzas stretching 1,630 ft (496 m) was laid out in 14 rows at Bucharest, Romania, in 2009. The pizza chain required 1,320 lb (600 kg) of flour, 880 lb (400 kg) of mozzarella, 440 lb (200 kg) of tomato sauce, 4 gal (15 l) of olive oil, and 6 lb 10 oz (3 kg) of yeast.

sundae lunch A London ice-cream parlor offered a new twist on the traditional British Sunday roast, with each course being a frozen dessert. The "Sundae Lunch," designed by Italian mixologist Roberto Lobrano, comprised a starter of fresh pea sorbet with mint, followed by a main course of beef bouillon and horseradish sorbet topped with a Yorkshire pudding wafer. The final course was an apple-and-blackberry-crumble gelato.

status symbols Pineapples were status symbols in 17th-century Britain, and wealthy people would rent them by the day to place on their dinner table and impress their friends.

big dipper Students from Miami-Dade, Florida, filled a 13-gal (49-l) bucket with homemade guacamole. The guacamole weighed 4,114 lb (1,866 kg) and was made from 3,500 lb (1,588 kg) of avocados, 500 lb (227 kg) of tomatoes, 100 lb (45 kg) of mayonnaise, and 500 limes.

lot of dough Using a secret 1950s sourdough recipe involving Somerset flour, Cotswolds spring water, and Cornish sea salt, baker Tom Herbert from Gloucestershire, England, creates loaves of bread that cost over $30 each. Each 4½-lb (2-kg) hand-crafted shepherd loaf takes him two days to make from start to finish.

MICE LUNCH

While making sandwiches for his family in 2010, a father from Oxfordshire, England, found an unwelcome ingredient in the bread he had bought from a local grocery store—a dead mouse baked into the half-eaten loaf. To make matters worse, the unfortunate rodent was missing its tail, leading Stephen Forse to wonder whether his family had already eaten it.

YUCKY FOOD FACTS

• For every 3½ oz (100 g) of product, the U.S. Food and Drug Administration allows a certain amount of alien material before taking action. This includes up to three rodent hairs and 60 insect fragments in chocolate, five fly eggs and one maggot in tomato juice, and one rodent hair and 30 insect parts in peanut butter.

• In 2010, an English chef opened a tin of baked beans and discovered a dead rat inside. Tests showed that it had not eaten any beans.

• A family from Kentucky drank from a container of milk for three days before they noticed that a mouse had died inside it.

• In 2009, a Florida man found an entire mouse inside his can of cola after complaining that it tasted strange.

chocolate fashion At the 15th Paris Salon du Chocolat in Shanghai, China, chefs and clothes designers from across the world combined their talents to create dresses, jackets, shoes, and handbags all made from chocolate.

edible plates To save on washing up after school dinners, catering boss Tiziano Vicentini from Milan, Italy, has devised a range of edible plates made from a kind of dough that is tough enough to last a lunchtime, but tasty enough to eat afterward.

Frog's Heart

Customers in Japan who order Frog Sashimi eat the still-beating heart of a freshly killed American bullfrog. The rest of the frog is eaten as a raw dish, with any leftovers, including the feet, turned into soup.

Ripley's Believe It or Not!®

Ripley's Believe It or Not!®

ACKNOWLEDGMENTS

COVER (t/l) Alex Smith - www.as-images.com, (b/l) Californiaskateparks.com, (r) Chin Boon Leng; 4 Jayna Sullivan Photography; 6–7 Alex Smith - www.as-images.com; 8 Getty Images; 9 (sp) Chin Boon Leng, (l) Reuters/Will Burgess; 10 Paul Christoforou; 11 (t) Richard Jones/Sinopix/ Rex Features, (b) Debbie Does Cakes/Rex Features; 12 Honda Motor Europe Ltd; 13 Californiaskateparks.com; 14 (l) EPA/Photoshot, (t/r) National Geographic/Getty Images, (b/r) Robyn Beck/AFP/Getty Images; 15 (t/l) SSPL via Getty Images, (t/r) Stephen L. Alvarez/National Geographic/ Getty Images, (b) Jae C. Hong/AP/Press Association Images; 16 (t) The Cheeky/Rex Features, (b) Wenn.com; 17 Barcroft Media; 18 Charles Eisenmann Collection/University of Syracuse; 19 Jayna Sullivan Photography; 20 (t) AP Photo, The Canadian Press, Lethbridge Herald, Ian Martens, (b) Gabriel Luque/Rex Features; 21 (t/l) AP Photo, The Canadian Press, Lethbridge Herald, Ian Martens, (t/r) Polaris/eyevine, (b/l, b/r) Rob Yuill/ Albanpix Ltd/Rex Features; 22 (t/l, t/r) Reuters/Reinhard Krause, (b/l) Collect/PA Wire/Press Association Images; 23 Getty Images; 24–25 Chris Trueman/Alexander Salazar Gallery; 26 (t) APOPO, (b/l) © EuroPics[CEN]; 27 (b/r) KeystoneUSA-ZUMA/Rex Features, (t/l, t/r) © EuroPics[CEN]; 28 (t/r, t/l) Getty Images, (b) From the John and Mable Ringling Museum of Art Tibbals Digital Collection; 29 (c, t/r) Charles Eisenmann Collection/ University of Syracuse, (b) Used with permission from Illinois State University's Special Collections, Milner Library; 31 (t) Jagdeep Rajput/Solent, (b) Theo Stroomer/Demotix; 32 Eddie Mitchell/Rex Features; 33 (t) INS News Agency Ltd./Rex Features, (b) Kevin Le; BACK COVER Honda Motor Europe Ltd

Key: t = top, b = bottom, c = center, l = left, r = right, sp = single page, dp = double page

All other photos are from Ripley Entertainment Inc.
Every attempt has been made to acknowledge correctly and contact copyright holders and we apologize in advance for any unintentional errors or omissions, which will be corrected in future editions.